Learning to Read, Step by Step!

Ready to Read   Preschool–Kindergarten
• big type and easy words • rhyme and rhythm • picture clues
For children who know the alphabet and are eager to begin reading.

Reading with Help   Preschool–Grade 1
• basic vocabulary • short sentences • simple stories
For children who recognize familiar words and sound out new words with help.

Reading on Your Own   Grades 1–3
• engaging characters • easy-to-follow plots • popular topics
For children who are ready to read on their own.

Reading Paragraphs   Grades 2–3
• challenging vocabulary • short paragraphs • exciting stories
For newly independent readers who read simple sentences with confidence.

Ready for Chapters   Grades 2–4
• chapters • longer paragraphs • full-color art
For children who want to take the plunge into chapter books but still like colorful pictures.

STEP INTO READING® is designed to give every child a successful reading experience. The grade levels are only guides; children will progress through the steps at their own speed, developing confidence in their reading. The F&P Text Level on the back cover serves as another tool to help you choose the right book for your child.

Remember, a lifetime love of reading starts with a single step!

To my lovely granddaughter Tamika Clay —W.C.

All rights reserved. Published in the United States by Random House Children's Books, a division of Penguin Random House LLC, New York. Originally published in hardcover in the United States by Dial Books for Young Readers, an imprint of Penguin Random House LLC, New York, in 1997.

Step into Reading, Random House, and the Random House colophon are registered trademarks of Penguin Random House LLC.

Art credits: Painting on p. 38 is based on a photograph used with permission of the Bettmann Archive. Painting on p. 39 is based on a photograph used with permission of the SCLC. Portrait of Mrs. Parks with children on p. 42 is based on a photograph © Monica Morgan/Monica Morgan Photography.

Visit us on the Web!
StepIntoReading.com
rhcbooks.com

Educators and librarians, for a variety of teaching tools, visit us at
RHTeachersLibrarians.com

Library of Congress Cataloging-in-Publication Data is available upon request.
ISBN 978-0-593-43272-3 (trade) — ISBN 978-0-593-43273-0 (lib. bdg.)

Printed in the United States of America
10 9 8 7 6 5 4 3 2 1

This book has been officially leveled by using the F&P Text Level Gradient™ Leveling System.

STEP INTO READING®

A BIOGRAPHY READER

I Am Rosa Parks

by Rosa Parks with Jim Haskins
illustrated by Wil Clay

Random House 🏠 New York

Contents

Chapter 1
I Get Arrested

Many years ago, black people in the South could not go to the same schools as white people. We could not eat in white restaurants. We could not even drink from the same water fountains.

We had to stay apart from white people everywhere we went. This was called segregation. Segregation was the law in the South. If we broke the law, we could be arrested or hurt or even killed.

When we rode a bus, we could only sit in the back seats. The front seats were just for white people.

If all the front seats were filled with
white people, we black people had
to give up our seats to the next white
people who got on the bus. That's the
way we rode the buses in the South when
I was younger.

I rode the buses and obeyed the laws that kept me apart from white people. But I did not think they were right.

One day I was riding on a bus. I was sitting in one of the seats in the back section for black people. The bus started to get crowded. The front seats filled up with white people. One white man was standing up.

The bus driver looked back at us black people sitting down.

The driver said, "Let me have those seats." He wanted us to get up and give our seats to white people.

But I was tired of doing that. I stayed in my seat.

This bus driver said to me, "I'm going to have you arrested."

"You may do that," I said. And I stayed in my seat.

Two policemen came. One asked me,
"Why didn't you stand up?"

I asked him, "Why do you push us
black people around?"

The policemen took me to jail. They took my picture. They put my fingers on a pad of ink and rolled my fingers onto white cards. That way, they had my fingerprints. Then they put me in a jail cell.

I did not have to spend the night in
the jail. My husband came to get me. A
friend paid my bail money. That meant I
could go free for now. The police told me
to come to court in three days.

I went to court. The judge said I was guilty of breaking the law. I was fined ten dollars, plus four dollars in court costs.

I never paid it.

I did not feel I had broken the law.
I thought black people should not have
to give up their seats on the bus to white
people. I thought the law should treat
black people and white people just the
same way. I always wanted rules to be
fair, even when I was small.

Chapter 2
How I Grew Up

I was born on February 4, 1913. I grew up in a place called Pine Level, Alabama. I was named Rosa Louise McCauley, after my grandma Rose.

My little brother was named Sylvester, after my grandpa. My mother's name was Leona. She was a schoolteacher. My father was a builder of houses. His name was James.

We lived on a farm with my grandma and grandpa. They owned their own land and grew vegetables and raised chickens on it.

I liked to go fishing with Grandma
and Grandpa. They could not see very
well, so I would put the worm on the
hook for them.

Pine Level was too small to have buses or public water fountains or even a library. But there was segregation just the same.

Sylvester and I went to a school for black children. It had only one room. White children went to a bigger school.

There was a school bus for the white children. There was no school bus for us.

Sometimes when we walked to school, the bus would go by carrying the white children. They would laugh at us and throw trash out the window. There was no way to stop them.

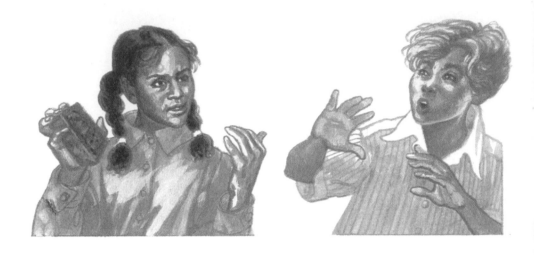

One day a white boy named Franklin tried to hit me. I picked up a brick, and I dared him to hit me. He went away.

My grandma was angry. She told me not to talk back to white folks. I thought I was right to talk back.

When I grew up, I married a man
named Raymond Parks. The year was
1932. He was a barber. He lived in the
city of Montgomery, Alabama.

I was proud of my husband because he worked to help black people. He helped get lawyers for people who had been arrested.

I began to work to help black people, too. I wrote down their stories when they were hurt by whites. I asked young black people to try to use the white library.

It was very hard work. It was also very sad work, because nothing we did really helped make our lives better.

Then came that day on the bus when
I would not give up my seat to a white
person. I was tired of black people being
pushed around.

Some people think I kept my seat
because I'd had a hard day, but that is
not true. I was just tired of giving in.

Chapter 3
We Stay Off the Buses

Many black people heard that I had been arrested. They were very angry. They thought it was time to fight for new laws.

A woman named Jo Ann Robinson
said we should not ride the buses if we
had to give up our seats to white people.
She passed out leaflets asking all black
people in the city of Montgomery to stay
off the buses for one day. This was called
a boycott.

The day of the boycott came. The buses were almost empty. Very few black people were on them.

A man named E. D. Nixon called a big
meeting of black people. The meeting
was held in a church. A young minister
named Dr. Martin Luther King, Jr.,
told all the black people to keep off the
buses.

Everyone at the meeting cheered, and
the boycott went on.

We walked to work or took taxis. We got rides from our friends. But we did not ride the buses.

Christmas passed. It was very cold, but we did not ride the buses.

White people were very angry. They wanted us to ride the buses again.

Some black people even lost their jobs because they would not ride the buses.

Some black people were arrested.
Some were beaten up.

I got telephone calls from people who
would not give their names. They said
they wanted to hurt me.

Spring came. Now it was nice weather for walking. All the black churches had station wagons to drive the people who could not walk.

Summer came. The buses had stopped running. There were not enough riders without the black people.

Mr. Nixon and Dr. King got lawyers
to take our case to court. They took our
case all the way to the Supreme Court in
Washington, D.C.

The Supreme Court said that the
segregation laws were wrong. Black
people should not have to give up their
bus seats to white people.

Our boycott worked, and we had won.
We went back to the buses at last. We did
not have to give up our seats anymore.
We had stayed off the buses for a whole
year.

Chapter 4
Since the Boycott

Many white people were angry that we had won. My brother was worried about our safety. My husband and I left Montgomery to find work and be near my brother. We moved up North, to Detroit, Michigan. My mother moved with us.

Back in the South, Dr. Martin Luther King, Jr., decided to fight against segregation in other ways. He led black people in the fight to vote and to eat in restaurants, just as white people did. He was fighting for their rights. This fight was called the civil rights movement.

Some white people joined the fight. Most went down South from the North. But some white people in the South joined the civil rights movement, too.

I helped out by making speeches. I told about being arrested. I went down South for some of the big marches for black people's rights.

The civil rights movement won many rights for black people. New laws for equal rights were passed. The old segregation laws were over.

Today I still make many speeches, and I receive many awards. Some people say I started the whole civil rights movement because I would not give up my seat on the bus.

I know that many people started the civil rights movement. And many people worked very hard to win the rights that black people have today. But I am glad that I did my part.

There is still much work to be done. The laws that kept black and white people apart have been changed. But there are still many people who have not changed their hearts.

I hope that children today will grow up without hate. I hope they will learn to respect one another, no matter what color they are.

A Note from the Editor

After this book was published, Rosa Parks received a very important award. It is called the Congressional Gold Medal. It is given by the United States Congress to a person who performs an outstanding deed or act of service. That describes what Rosa Parks did when she refused to give up her seat!

And in 2000, the city of Montgomery, Alabama, opened the Rosa Parks Library and Museum. It is in the same spot where Rosa was arrested in 1955.

Rosa Parks died on October 24, 2005. She was 92 years old. After she died, her casket was placed in the rotunda of the Capitol building in Washington, D.C. This was a very big honor. Something like this usually only happens when a president dies. Rosa's casket stayed in the room for two days. People came from all over to say good-bye.

Today, people in the United States can sit wherever they want on buses—no matter who they are. Rosa Parks is a powerful example of how the actions of one person can make a big difference.

Timeline of Rosa Parks's Life

1913 Rosa Louise McCauley is born in Tuskegee, Alabama

1932 Rosa marries Raymond Parks

1955 Rosa is arrested for refusing to give up her seat on a bus to a white man

People of Montgomery, Alabama, refuse to ride the buses

1956 Montgomery Bus Boycott ends

1957 Rosa and Raymond move to Detroit, Michigan

1996 Rosa is given the Presidential Medal of Freedom by President Bill Clinton

1999 Rosa is given the Congressional Gold Medal

2000 Rosa Parks Library and Museum is opened in Montgomery, Alabama

2005 Rosa Parks dies